4/95

QUINCEAÑERA

Quinceañera

A Latina's Journey to Womanhood

BY MARY D. LANKFORD

Photographs by Jesse Herrera

The Millbrook Press
Brookfield, Connecticut

Library of Congress Cataloging-in-Publication Data

Lankford, Mary D.
Quinceanera : a Latina's journey to womanhood
by Mary D. Lankford : photographs by Jesse Herrera.
p.   cm.
Includes bibliographical references and index.
ISBN 1-56294-363-4 (lib. bdg.)
1. Quinceanera—Juvenile literature.   I. Herrera, Jesse.
II. Title.
GT2490.L36   1994
395'.24—dc20   93-1260   CIP   AC

Published by The Millbrook Press
2 Old New Milford Road
Brookfield, Connecticut 06804

Acknowledgments

For encouragement and newspaper citations from librarians in Austin, Texas, Elizabeth Polk, June Kahler, and Elizabeth Haines;

For newspaper citations from California, Beverly Braun;

For sharing a bibliography, Kathy Seymour;

For continued support of librarians at Irving Public Library, Julie Judd, Laurie Chase, Genevieve Ramos, Delfina Lerma;

For an informative interview and for scholarly research, Sister Angela Erevia, MCDP;

For sharing memories of their quinceañeras, Maria Flores Williams and Marta Patricia Rodriguez;

For taking time to interview and provide information about the quinceañera in Guatemala, Ann Cameron;

For the assistance of El Paso librarians Shirley Bowie and Linda Rivera.

A special thank you to Oralia Garza de Cortes who suggested Jesse Herrera as the photographer.

More than a thank you is due to Gail Green, librarian at Brandenburg Elementary School, Irving, Texas. It was at her school that I first saw a visual display of the quinceañera. Gail provided the idea that aroused my curiosity.

Editor's Note: Latina or Hispanic?

In deciding whether to refer to Martha Jimenez—the girl whose quinceañera this book presents—as a Latina or as a Hispanic, Mary Lankford and I considered carefully the implications of each of these terms.
We were aware that to some people the term Latino or Latina has a
negative connotation, conjuring stereotypical images of populations
from Cuba, Puerto Rico, Central and Latin America. These people
prefer the term Hispanic. We also understood that others view Hispanic as a term erasing the ethnicity of groups more properly referred
to as Latinos. We were unable to find any consensus on this matter.
We opted for Latina, therefore, while keeping in mind that any at-
tempt to yoke together Spanish-speaking peoples living in the United
States under a single name ultimately ignores their profound cultural
differences.

Frank Menchaca

Dedicated to Catie Morgan
Who perceives the person not the façade

Contents

Introduction:
From a Girl to a Woman

🐘 *Rites of Passage* 🐘

Our journeys through life include many personal changes. We grow; our bodies change. We change our minds: Things we enjoyed doing at age nine we would never dream of doing at age twelve.

Frequently we recognize life's important personal changes with celebrations. Birthday parties, for example, celebrate changes in age.

Adolescence is a time of great personal change. During adolescence, girls and boys pass from childhood into adulthood, going on to become young women and men. Throughout history and all over the world, people have acknowledged the special status of such changes between phases of life not only with celebrations, but with elaborate ceremonies.

These ceremonies, called *rites of passage*, are created by societies, religions, and other institutions. In the Native American Navajo society of the southwestern United States, young girls experience the rite of passage known as *Kinaalda*. In this rite, girls endure physical tests that help shape the body and spirit for adulthood. The rite of passage celebrating the move to adulthood of thirteen-year-old Jewish boys is called a *bar mitzvah*. Jewish girls at age twelve or thirteen have a similar rite of passage called a *bat mitzvah*.

Quinceañera

For girls of Latino background, whether they, or their parents, were born in Mexico, Cuba, Puerto Rico, or Latin America, the fifteenth birthday is an occasion for a rite of passage called *quinceañera*. This rite traces its history to the ancient native American cultures of Central and Latin America, and particularly Mexico.

In Mexico's Native American Aztec civilization, girls of twelve or thirteen attended two types of schools, the *Calmacac* or the *Telpucucali*. Those who entered the *Calmacac* school prepared for a lifetime of religious service. Girls who enrolled in the *Telpucucali* school prepared for marriage. The initiation rites for girls in both schools stressed chastity, truthfulness, and obedience.

After the Spanish conquered the Aztecs in 1521, the traditions of their Catholic religion meshed with the initiation rites of the Aztecs. As these rites continued to develop, the age of fifteen marked a time of decision for young women. Their choice was between a lifetime of service to the church, or marriage. These rites received the name quinceañera from the Spanish words for fifteen, *quince*, and birthday, *años*.

Today the celebration of the fifteenth birthday, or quinceañera, of many Latino girls represents a rite of passage from childhood to adulthood. It affirms religious faith *and* celebrates entrance into womanhood. The ceremony may be as simple as a reaffirmation of baptismal vows in church and a party in the backyard, or as elaborate as a large wedding.

In this book, we will witness the quinceañera of a Mexican girl who lives in Austin, Texas. We will follow her through the many months of planning her quinceañera up to the day on which, in front of family, friends, and religious leaders, she graduates from the religious education of childhood and begins her journey from girlhood to womanhood.

MARTHA'S QUINCEAÑERA

Planning for Womanhood

At the time of her quinceañera, Martha Jimenez was in the eighth grade at Porter Middle School in Austin, Texas. Martha was born in Mexico and moved with her family to the United States when she was seven weeks old.

Martha spent more than a year planning for her quinceañera. First she and her parents set a date for the event. Although the quinceañera celebrates a girl's fifteenth birthday, it is often held days, weeks, or even months after the actual birthday to allow out-of-town friends and relatives to attend.

Many questions about the ceremony at the church and the party afterward had to be answered. What music would be played? At church, there would be a choir singing hymns of faith in Spanish. The music at the party would serve one purpose: to get everyone—young and old—to dance.

It is customary for a girl undergoing a quinceañera to have an escort for the day and a group of attendants. This group, called a *corte de honor,* or court of honor, consists of pairs of boys and girls. The boys are called *chambelánes,* or lords, and the girls are *damas,* or ladies. Together with the girl and her escort, the total number of couples is usually fifteen—each couple representing a year to be celebrated. Martha put much thought into choosing the members of her *corte*.

Martha and her parents had to make decisions about the party. What food and drink would be served? Invitations had to be printed and addressed. There were so many details to see to that Martha and her mother kept lists of things to do, as well as a calendar showing the dates that were critical in the decision-making process.

Because both the church service and the celebration involved the participation of family and friends, Martha and her parents discussed their ideas before making any decisions. In fact, quinceañeras are often the results of the decisions and work of many people—extended family members and friends. Because of the expense of a celebration of this size, friends and relatives often assist in the planning and share in the expense.

The counseling sessions Martha and her parents attended at their church also stressed the importance of family and community in the religious rites of the quinceañera. At one point, Martha's mother was asked to write down her feelings about her daughter and read them aloud to her. When she heard her mother's words of confidence in her as she approached womanhood, Martha embraced her mother.

Last but certainly not least, Martha decided what she and her attendants would wear. Clothing for the young men was simple. They had to be fitted for rented tuxedoes. Dresses for all of the *damas* had to be made, however, and required many fittings. The girls gathered at Martha's house to discuss dress patterns and fabrics.

Martha traveled with her family to Durango, Mexico, to purchase her dress. As so often happens with girls celebrating quinceañeras, Martha's dress became, for a time, her most precious possession.

To the Church

After months of preparation, the big event came.

Small groups of family and friends gathered on the steps of the San Jose Catholic Church where the mass was to be held, waiting for Martha. The car, decorated by the *chambelánes* with crepe-paper streamers and rosettes, arrived. Cameras clicked as Martha emerged and walked the few steps from the car to the church entrance.

Martha's face was filled with calm anticipation. The beautiful white lace and satin dress flared from her small waist down to a floor-length circular skirt. An unknowing spectator might have described her as a fairy princess, or young bride. As she cast a backward glance before entering the church, perhaps her thoughts focused not only on the events of the day, but on her responsibilities of the future.

In the lobby or vestibule of the church, twenty-eight *damas* and *chambelánes* smiled self-consciously as they received final instructions and flowers from a woman coordinating the ceremony. The young men, dressed in black tuxedoes with pink cummerbunds and bow ties, were handsome and shy. The young women, who wore off-the-shoulder pink satin dresses, had been transformed from giggling girls to poised young ladies who walked arm and arm with their escorts into the church.

Promises of Faith

The ceremony began as the fourteen couples proceeded down the aisle followed by Martha and her parents. The attendants walked to the front of the church. At the first pew, the line of couples divided as boys sat to the right and girls to the left. Martha and her parents took their places to the right of the priest.

Martha then received from her parents a necklace. This, with the rosary and prayer book she carried, reflected the continuity of the relationship between her church and family. Next, as a sign of her faith, Martha placed a rose in a bouquet beneath the altar of Our Lady of Guadalupe, Mexico's patron saint.

The music throughout the Mass was a blend of voices and guitar. Spanish words and rhythms filled the church with praise and thanksgiving.

The quinceañera mass is not just a religious service. It is a reaffirmation of promises of religious faith, bringing together all of the religious rites a girl has already undergone. Martha's baptism symbolized her parents' promise to educate her within the church. When Martha participated in the Eucharist, or celebrated Holy Communion, accepting the bread and water symbolized her faith in Christ's resurrection. Her confirmation renewed the promise of the importance of religious faith in her life. In her quinceañera mass, Martha reaffirmed her baptismal and confirmation vows and accepted the Eucharist, rededicating herself to the spiritual aspects of life.

At the conclusion of the Mass, Martha and her parents, arms linked, left the church followed by the court of honor.

The Pause Before the Party

There were many out-of-town family members and friends who ate lunch in Martha's home. The small, neat house was crowded with family enjoying the hospitality of the Jimenez family. Everyone continued to wear their party clothes throughout the day. Martha, her dark hair cascading over her shoulders, was patient with the younger children seeking her attention. Her soft voice moved easily from English to Spanish.

The Fiesta

As family and friends arrived at the community hall in the evening, the young men and women serving in the court of honor completed a final rehearsal of the traditional first dance of the party. The lawn between the church and the community building served as a dance floor. The first dance, a waltz, involved turning the partner under upraised arms.

Inside the hall final preparations were made. A sign in Spanish read: Welcome to Martha's 15th Birthday. Balloons and flowers decorated the hall. A flower-covered archway was placed opposite a high-backed wicker chair.

The delicious smells of food drifted from the back of the room. A buffet provided guests with a variety of spicy Mexican food. The multi-tiered birthday cake included a lighted fountain. The aroma, the sights, and the excitement were all heightened by the sounds of musicians testing their instruments and sound system.

The Dance

The attendants entered the dance floor through the archway and formed a corridor for Martha and her escort. The couple was followed by Martha's parents. Martha's mother carried a white satin pillow. On top of the pillow rested a pair of white high-heeled shoes. Martha, still smiling, sat in the high-backed chair. Her father knelt in front of her and placed the shoes on her feet. The shoes were yet another symbol of Martha's move from childhood to young adulthood and of her entrance into the dance of life. She rose from her chair and danced one dance with her father.

Her father then stepped aside so she could dance with her escort, the *chambelán de honor*, Jesus Benitez. The couple waltzed, gliding and turning as they danced down the court of honor. The crisscross dance pattern allowed Martha to have one turn with her escort and each of the *chambelánes*. The *chambelán de honor*, following the first dance with Martha, danced a turn with each of the *damas*.

Close family ties and community spirit were obvious. The dress of the guests was unimportant. The joy of the moment prevailed as the music called everyone to join in the dance. There was no segregation by age. Even off the dance floor, the merriment continued.

The remainder of the evening the youngest and the oldest danced. Everyone made several trips to the buffet to enjoy the generous offering of food.

The party and the dancers were a beautiful blend of cultures, family, and friends. The sights and sounds of this evening were not just about Martha Jimenez; they were signs, symbols, and songs of how young Latinas move from their carefree girlhood into the choice-filled world of womanhood.

Ritual acts like the quinceañera commemorate events in our lives that are very important. Gifts received as a part of the commemoration of a fifteenth birthday may be lost, but the events of the quinceañera day will forever remain in the memory.

Martha will continue to reflect back on childhood through her memories and through the activities of those younger than herself. Through her quinceañera she has taken the first steps in a journey forward into womanhood and into the new life that has opened before her.

Further Reading

Cohen, David. *The Circle of Life: Rituals from the Human Family*. San Francisco: HarperCollins San Francisco, 1991.

Erevia, Sister Angela. *Quince Años: Celebrating a Tradition*. San Antonio, Texas: Missionary Catechists of Divine Providence, 1985.

Kalman, Bobby. *We Celebrate Family Days*. New York: Crabtree Publishing, 1986.

Milinaire, Catherine. *Celebrations from Birth to Death and From New Year's to Christmas*. New York: Harmony Books, 1981.

Odijk, Pamela. *The Aztecs*. New York: Franklin Watts, 1990.

Index

About the Author

Mary D. Lankford is Director of Library and Media Services for the Irving Public Schools in Irving, Texas. She is the author of the books *Is it Dark? Is it Light?*, *Hopscotch Around the World*, and *Christmas Customs Around the World*, all for children. Her books for teachers include: *Successful Field Trips*, and *Films for Learning, Thinking and Doing*.

About the Photographer

Jesse Herrera is a documentary photographer with a special interest in religious ceremonies in Mexico and Spain. He became interested in photography while stationed in Da Nang during the Vietnam War. He has a master's degree in photography from the University of Texas and his photographs have appeared in many exhibitions and Spanish-language publications.